EGYPTIAN MYTHOLOGY

ISIS

BY ALYSSA KREKELBERG

CONTENT CONSULTANT
KASIA SZPAKOWSKA, PhD
PROFESSOR EMERITUS OF EGYPTOLOGY

Kids Core
An Imprint of Abdo Publishing
abdobooks.com

abdobooks.com

Published by Abdo Publishing, a division of ABDO, PO Box 398166, Minneapolis, Minnesota 55439. Copyright © 2023 by Abdo Consulting Group, Inc. International copyrights reserved in all countries. No part of this book may be reproduced in any form without written permission from the publisher. Kids Core™ is a trademark and logo of Abdo Publishing.

Printed in the United States of America, North Mankato, Minnesota.
052022
092022

THIS BOOK CONTAINS RECYCLED MATERIALS

Cover Photos: Shutterstock Images, desert; Olga Chernyak/Shutterstock Images, Isis
Interior Photos: Shutterstock Images, 4–5, 8, 10–11, 25 (top right), 25 (bottom left), 28 (top), 28 (bottom); Sepia Times/Universal Images Group/Getty Images, 6, 29 (top); Graficam Ahmed Saeed/Shutterstock Images, 12; Bas Photo/Shutterstock Images, 14; The Print Collector/Alamy, 16; Nastasic/Digital Vision Vectors/Getty Images, 18–19; Nestor Noci/Shutterstock Images, 21; Unai Huizi Photography/Shutterstock Images, 22; Alexander P/Shutterstock Images, 25 (top left); Masahiro Suzuki/Shutterstock Images, 25 (bottom right); Robert Paul Van Beets/Shutterstock Images, 26, 29 (bottom)

Editor: Layna Darling
Series Designer: Ryan Gale

Library of Congress Control Number: 2021952324

Publisher's Cataloging-in-Publication Data

Names: Krekelberg, Alyssa, author.
Title: Isis / by Alyssa Krekelberg
Description: Minneapolis, Minnesota : Abdo Publishing, 2023 | Series: Egyptian mythology | Includes online resources and index.
Identifiers: ISBN 9781532198687 (lib. bdg.) | ISBN 9781644947760 (pbk.) | ISBN 9781098272333 (ebook)
Subjects: LCSH: Isis (Egyptian deity)--Juvenile literature. | Egypt--Religion--Juvenile literature. | Gods, Egyptian--Juvenile literature. | Mythology, Egyptian--Juvenile literature.
Classification: DDC 932.01--dc23

CONTENTS

Isis is one of the most well-known Egyptian goddesses.

PROTECTING HER SON

The goddess Isis walked through the marshes of the Nile River. She held her son, Horus, close to her chest. She was hiding from the cruel god Seth. He was looking for her and Horus. He wanted to hurt Horus.

Isis was known for her magical powers. This illustration shows her in a protective pose with wings outspread.

the world came to be. To help answer these questions, the ancient Egyptians told stories of powerful gods and goddesses. Today, these stories are known as Egyptian myths.

Isis was one of the most important goddesses in Egyptian mythology. She was known for her magical powers. She was the goddess of **fertility**, motherhood, healing, death, and rebirth. Ancient Egyptians viewed Isis as the perfect mother. Many people worshipped her.

Explore Online

Visit the website below. Does it give any new information about Isis that wasn't in Chapter One?

Isis and Osiris

abdocorelibrary.com/isis

Isis was known for her magical powers. This illustration shows her in a protective pose with wings outspread.

PROTECTING HER SON

The goddess Isis walked through the **marshes** of the Nile River. She held her son, Horus, close to her chest. She was hiding from the cruel god Seth. He was looking for her and Horus. He wanted to hurt Horus.

Ancient Egyptians told stories about many gods and goddesses. These myths explained events in their society.

The ancient Egyptians had a thriving **culture**. They asked many questions about the world. They were curious about what happened after people died. They also wondered how had magical healing powers. She cured him every time.

What Is Egyptian Mythology?

Ancient Egypt was a civilization that existed around 5,000 years ago. Many cities formed along the Nile River in Africa. A pharaoh, or king, ruled over them.

The Seven Scorpions

Some stories say seven scorpions protected Isis and Horus. Once, Isis and Horus went to a town to look for food. Isis begged a rich woman for help. The woman refused. The angry scorpions poisoned the woman's son. Seeing the child in danger upset Isis. She used her powers to save him.

Ancient Egyptians told stories about many gods and goddesses. These myths explained events in their society.

The ancient Egyptians had a thriving **culture**. They asked many questions about the world. They were curious about what happened after people died. They also wondered how

PROTECTING HER SON

The goddess Isis walked through the **marshes** of the Nile River. She held her son, Horus, close to her chest. She was hiding from the cruel god Seth. He was looking for her and Horus. He wanted to hurt Horus.

Isis was married to the god of the underworld, Osiris. Together they had a son, Horus.

Isis used to rule Egypt with her husband, the god Osiris. But Seth grew jealous of Osiris and killed him. Now, Seth wanted to make sure Horus couldn't take the throne away from him. Isis hid in the wild to protect Horus. The child faced many dangers there. He was bitten by crocodiles, scorpions, and snakes. But Isis

CHAPTER 2

MYTHS ABOUT ISIS

Isis was the daughter of the sky goddess, Nut, and the earth god, Geb. Isis married Osiris, and the two of them ruled Egypt. They wanted to teach people about the importance of government, religion, and marriage. Isis was known for her healing powers.

The Nile River played an important role in ancient Egyptian society. Today, it still provides food, resources, and more.

She shared her magical knowledge with the Egyptians.

Finding Osiris

Isis wasn't there when Seth attacked her husband. Seth trapped Osiris in a coffin.

He threw the coffin into the Nile River. When Isis learned what had happened, she was heartbroken. She looked all over Egypt for her husband. When she finally found Osiris, he was dead. But Isis thought she could bring Osiris back to life with her magical powers. She took his body home.

The Most Important Goddess

Isis is the Greek spelling of the goddess's name. In ancient Egypt, she was known as Aset. At first, ancient Egyptians saw Isis as less important than Osiris. As time went on, more stories were told of her great power. She became the most valued of all the gods and goddesses in ancient Egypt.

Isis, *right*, was seen as the perfect wife to Osiris, *left*. She protected him and their child.

Seth now ruled Egypt. When he discovered that Isis had found her husband's body, Seth took the body. He spread pieces of Osiris all over Egypt. That didn't stop Isis though.

She turned herself into a bird and found most of the pieces. She bandaged Osiris together. Osiris woke up, but he wasn't truly living or dead. He couldn't stay on earth. Instead, he had to go to the underworld. But before he left, Isis became pregnant with their son, Horus. She promised to protect him from the cruel Seth.

Tricking Ra

Isis wanted to strengthen her magical skills. But she needed the true name of the powerful creator god, Ra, to do this. Ra was getting old. He often drooled. One day, Isis collected some of his spit. She mixed it with dirt and turned it into a snake. Then she left it on a road Ra often walked.

An image from British artist Evelyn Paul shows Isis asking Ra to tell her his name.

When Ra passed by, the snake attacked. It sank its fangs into the god and poisoned him. No one knew how to help him except Isis. She pretended that she didn't know what had poisoned Ra. She watched as Ra began to drip with sweat and lose his eyesight. She told Ra that she could save him, but only if he told her his true name. When Ra gave it to her, she saved him. With Ra's true name, Isis became even more powerful.

Isis was known as a protective wife. **Egyptologist** L. V. Žabkar translated this hymn about her:

> Praise to you, Isis, the Great-One,
>
> God's Mother, Lady of Heaven, queen of the gods.
>
> You are the First Royal Spouse of [Osiris],
>
> One who protects her brother, and watches over the weary-of-heart.

Source: L. V. Žabkar. "Six Hymns to Isis in the Sanctuary of Her Temple at Philae." *Journal of Egyptian Archaeology*, vol. 69, no. 1, 1983, jstor.org. 115–37.

What's the Big Idea?

Read this quote. Does it support the information in this chapter? Explain how in a few sentences.

Isis, *left*, was often considered the mother of Egyptian pharaohs like Seti I, *right*.

CHAPTER 3

ISIS IN ANCIENT EGYPT

Isis was well-known in ancient times. Ancient Egyptians thought Isis helped people with childbirth, fertility, healing, and love. They also believed she protected them after they died. Isis was seen as the defender of women and pharaohs.

The Perfect Mother

Ancient Egyptians valued motherhood. They viewed Isis as a perfect mother. They honored her for her healing powers and for protecting her son.

Many stories told of Horus getting hurt by crocodiles, scorpions, and snakes. These creatures were real threats to ancient Egyptians' children too. Egyptians tried to treat their injured children the same way Isis did. They made medicine. They spoke what they believed were magical spells that would heal their children.

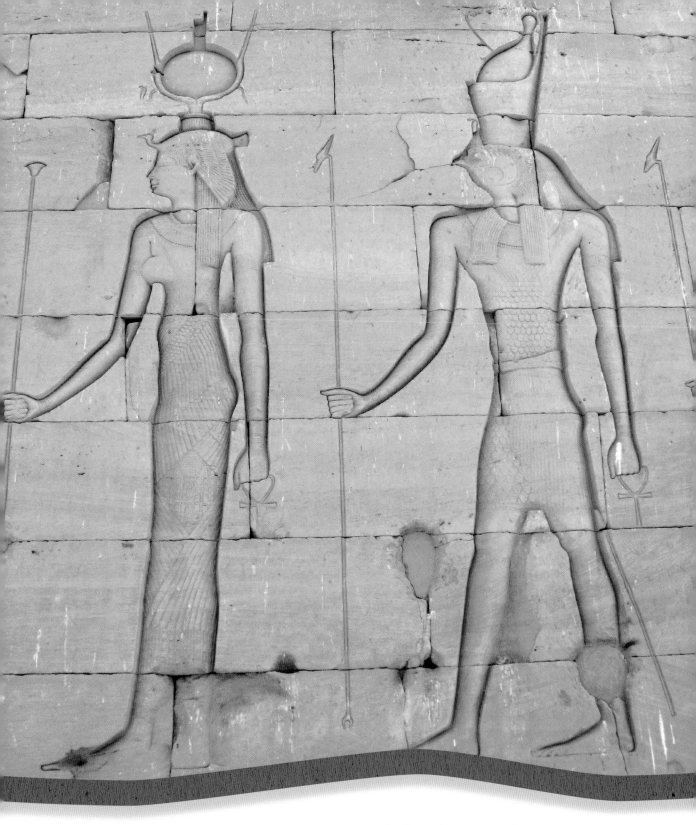

The walls of the Temple of Kalabsha show myths about Isis.

Today, people in Egypt can still see the Temple of Philae.

Worshipping the Goddess

People built temples to honor Isis. One is on the Egyptian island Philae. It's called the Temple of Isis. People can visit it today.

The walls of the temple are decorated with scenes of famous myths about Isis. They show Isis bringing Osiris back to life. They also show her giving birth to Horus. Ancient Egyptians visited the temple and left offerings to Isis. They did this to express to Isis that they respected her. Many would leave offerings of small bronze statues of the goddess.

Widespread Worship

People have found evidence that Isis was well-known beyond Egypt. They know the goddess was worshipped along the Mediterranean coast, in places known today as Syria, Turkey, and Israel. Temples for Isis were built in Greek cities such as Athens. They were also in Roman cities such as Pompeii.

Isis in Artwork

Isis is a popular figure in ancient Egyptian artwork. She's shown as a lovely woman wearing a dress. Isis is often seen with an Egyptian symbol on her head. This represents her Egyptian name, Aset. Some say it also represents her connection to Egyptian pharaohs. The ancient Egyptians saw Isis as the mother to all pharaohs.

Oftentimes, small statues of Isis show her sitting or standing on a throne. She holds Horus in her arms. These statues were very popular in ancient Egypt. They show Isis as a protector and as a life giver. Sometimes she is kneeling with wings outspread. The wings also represent safekeeping.

Symbols of the Goddess

Bird

One myth says that Isis temporarily turned into a bird after Osiris died. The noises she made in her bird form sounded like sad cries.

Throne

Isis was connected to the throne of Egypt. The ancient Egyptian pharaohs were said to have all been related to Isis.

Tit Amulet

The tit **amulet** was also known as the Isis knot. Ancient Egyptians made them out of stone. When a person died, they put one near the body's neck. They hoped the amulet would protect the person in the afterlife.

Sirius

The star Sirius was connected with Isis because of her status as the goddess of fertility. Sirius would appear in the sky each year before the Nile River flooded. Egyptian land depended on the floods for fertile soil.

The Egyptians connected a few important symbols to Isis.

The Romans built a temple to honor Isis in Pompeii. The remains still stand today.

The ancient Egyptians valued Isis for being a loving wife and mother. They believed she had power over them both while they were alive and after they died. The ancient Egyptians honored her by building temples and creating beautiful artwork in her image. They told stories about her that live on today.

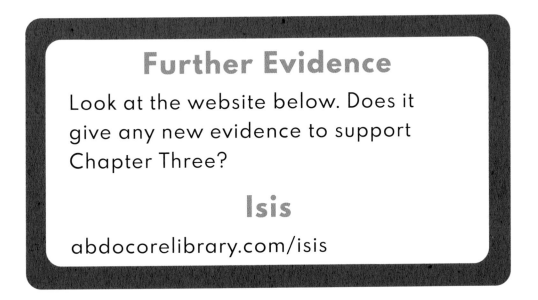

Further Evidence

Look at the website below. Does it give any new evidence to support Chapter Three?

Isis

abdocorelibrary.com/isis

LEGENDARY FACTS

Isis was the goddess of fertility, motherhood, healing, death, and rebirth.

Isis had magical healing powers. She used them to heal her son's injuries and bring back her husband after Seth killed him.

Ancient Egyptians viewed Isis as the perfect mother.

Isis's myths spread far beyond Egypt. Some ancient people in the Middle East and Europe worshipped her too.

Glossary

amulet
a small object believed to protect against danger or evil

civilization
a complex, organized society

culture
the customs, traditions, ideas, and ways of life shared by a group of people

Egyptologist
a person who studies the history and culture of ancient Egypt

fertility
the ability to create life and support growth

marshes
areas of muddy, wet land

Online Resources

To learn more about Isis, visit our free resource websites below.

Visit **abdocorelibrary.com** or scan this QR code for free Common Core resources for teachers and students, including vetted activities, multimedia, and booklinks, for deeper subject comprehension.

Visit **abdobooklinks.com** or scan this QR code for free additional online weblinks for further learning. These links are routinely monitored and updated to provide the most current information available.

Learn More

Bell, Samantha S. *Osiris*. Abdo, 2023.

Flynn, Sarah Wassner. *Ancient Egypt*. National Geographic, 2019.

Index

About the Author

Alyssa Krekelberg has been fascinated with Egyptian mythology since elementary school. She lives in Minnesota, where she writes and edits books for young readers.